DEDICATION

I dedicate this book to my fellow dreamers. May these affirmations be a spark that encourages you to dream even bigger, reaching heights you never thought possible.

Dream On Dreamers

A Poem Written By Darius Hubbard

THE SKY IS NOT THE LIMIT

POSITIVE AFFIRMATIONS
TO HELP YOU RISE ABOVE THE SKY

BY NICHOLAS BUAMAH

ISBN: 978-1-7330681-9-2
Library of Congress Control Number: 2024901392

Printed in the United States of America
First Printing 2024
Mother Hubbard & Co. LLC
3375 Centerville Hwy #391385
Snellville, GA 30039

Instagram.com/NicholasBuamah
Facebook.com/NicholasBuamah

Only Birds Can Fly They Told Him
But Deep In His Heart, He Knew They Were Wrong
He Knew He Could Fly With The Eagles
For In The Sky Was Where He Belonged
Stop Being Such A Dreamer
The Many Doubters Said
But Dream
Was The Only Word
That Ever Reached His Head
Do You Really Think You're Special
Deep In His Heart He Knew That He Was
Do You Really Think You Can Do It
Deep In His Soul He Knew That He Must
Early One Morning Half Thinking
He Opened His Arms, And Began To Run
Only Birds Can Fly
They Told Him He Thought
As He Flew Into The Sun

BY: DARIUS HUBBARD
(DREAM ALI)

Flip This Book

SINGLE-SIDED AFFIRMATIONS FOR EASY REMOVAL AND FRAMING

The WORLD IS MY CANVAS

AND WITH EACH

STROKE

I PAINT A MASTERPIECE OF

LIMITLESS

OPPORTUNITIES

THE SKY WILL BE MY STEPPINGSTONE TO GREATER ACHIEVEMENTS

THE SKY IS NOT MY LIMIT

IT'S MY LAUNCHPAD TO A UNIVERSE OF EXCITING OPPORTINITIES

I Will Not Limit

MY CREATIVITY

Because of someone else's

INABILITY To Dream

Bigger!

OTHERS' GLASS CEILINGS transform into my transparent floor PROPELLING ME Upward towards the fulfillment of my Dreams

YOU ARE ONLY CONFINED BY THE BOUNDARIES OF WHAT YOU BELIEVE YOU CAN ACHIEVE

ACHIEVING

GREAT HEIGHTS IS REMARKABLE

BUT MY DREAMS KNOW

No Limits!

Reaching the SKY
IS AN AMAZING FEAT
BUT MY DREAMS ARE
Limitless

I WILL PUSH PAST MY LIMITS and SHOW THAT ANYTHING IS POSSIBLE

I DICTATE My Own Level of SUCCESS

CAN'T STOP! WON'T STOP! DON'T STOP!

Your Potential Knows
NO LIMIT

The World
IS MY
PLAYGROUND
I see endless opportunities
At Every
TURN

Reaching The Sky Is Just The Beginning

DREAM BIG!

NEVER STOP DREAMING

I AM THE
ARCHITECT
OF MY DESTINY
CREATING PATHWAYS TO LIMITLESS
OPPORTUNITIES

AS I ASCEND

I LEAVE BEHIND THE NOTION

THAT THE SKY

IS MY ULTIMATE DESTINATION

YOU'RE only
LIMITED
BY WHAT YOU BELIEVE
YOU CAN ACCOMPLISH

UNBREAKABLE

UNSTOPPABLE

NO LIMITS

YOUR DREAMS

Await Above The

SKY

EACH DAY
I Strive To Surpass
MY OWN
Expectations

My Dreams

Are Not Mere Fantasies they are blueprints OF A FUTURE OF EXTRAORDINARY Achievements

I AM LIMITLESS

AND MY DREAMS ARE BOUNDLESS

There Is
NO LIMIT
To Your
GREATNESS

AFFIRMATION CARD
CUT-OUTS

Cut and carry affirmation cards.
Share them with others, and let the power of
positive words enhance your daily journey.

The WORLD IS MY CANVAS
AND WITH EACH STROKE
I PAINT A MASTERPIECE OF
LIMITLESS OPPORTUNITIES

THE *SKY* **WILL BE MY STEPPINGSTONE** TO *GREATER* **ACHIEVEMENTS**

THE SKY IS NOT MY **LIMIT**
IT'S MY LAUNCHPAD TO A UNIVERSE OF EXCITING OPPORTINITIES

I Will Not Limit
MY CREATIVITY
Because of
someone else's
INABILITY **To Dream**
Bigger!

....

OTHERS' **GLASS CEILINGS**

transform into my transparent floor

PROPELLING ME *Upward*

towards the fulfillment of my

Dreams

....

YOU ARE ONLY CONFINED

BY THE BOUNDARIES

OF WHAT YOU BELIEVE YOU CAN

ACHIEVE

ACHIEVING
GREAT HEIGHTS IS REMARKABLE
BUT MY DREAMS KNOW
No Limits!

Reaching the SKY
IS AN AMAZING FEAT
BUT MY DREAMS ARE
Limitless

I WILL
PUSH
PAST MY LIMITS
SHOW THAT ANYTHING IS
POSSIBLE

I DICTATE My Own Level of SUCCESS

CAN'T STOP!
WON'T STOP!
DON'T STOP!

Your Potential Knows NO LIMIT

The World IS MY PLAYGROUND

I see endless opportunities

At Every TURN

Reaching The Sky Is Just The BEGINNING

DREAM BIG!

NEVER STOP DREAMING

I AM THE
ARCHITECT
OF MY DESTINY
CREATING PATHWAYS TO LIMITLESS
OPPORTUNITIES

- -

AS I ASCEND

I LEAVE BEHIND THE NOTION

THAT THE SKY

IS MY ULTIMATE DESTINATION

- -

UNBREAKABLE
UNSTOPPABLE
NO LIMITS

YOUR
DREAMS
await Above The
SKY

EACH DAY
I Strive To Surpass
MY OWN
Expectations

My
Dreams
Are Not Mere Fantasies
they are blueprints OF
A FUTURE OF EXTRAORDINARY
Achievements

I AM
LIMITLESS
AND MY DREAMS
ARE BOUNDLESS

There Is
NO LIMIT
To Your
GREATNESS

TIME FOR REFLECTION

Describe a time when you
pushed beyond your limits.
How did it make you feel?

Imagine yourself soaring
above the clouds. What
limitless possibilities do
you see for your future?

Reflect on a goal that
once seemed out of
reach. How can you
break it down into
smaller, achievable
steps?

NOTES

Write about a challenge you've overcome and how it has contributed to your personal growth.

Consider the phrase "no limits." What areas of your life can benefit from adopting this mindset?

Explore a dream or aspiration you've hesitated to pursue. What steps can you take today to move closer to it?

Visualize yourself achieving a major success. How does it empower you to aim even higher?

NOTES

Write about a passion or talent you possess that you haven't fully embraced. How can you nurture it further?

Picture yourself standing at the edge of your comfort zone. What's one step you can take to venture beyond it?

Reflect on a time when you faced self-doubt. How did you overcome it, and what did you learn?

NOTES

Write a letter to your future self, envisioning the incredible achievements you've accomplished.

Consider the concept of limitless potential. How does it inspire you to set bolder goals?

NOTES

Explore the idea of resilience. Share a story of how you bounced back from adversity and grew stronger.

Imagine a world where fear doesn't exist. How would you approach your goals differently?

NOTES

MY JOURNEY HAS JUST BEGUN!

NICHOLAS BUAMAH

FLY

Far up in the sky
Something amazing awaits
When you finally arrive, what will you do
Will you stay, admiring the beauty
Or will you soar to new heights
Where you're destined to shine even brighter
The choice is yours
But tell me now
Are you ready to fly

BY: NICHOLAS BUAMAH

AUTHOR

NICHOLAS BUAMAH

AUTHOR – PRODUCER – PHILANTHROPIST

Nicholas Buamah is a 12-year-old author, producer, and philanthropist with an impressive portfolio. The young author has four books published and cataloged in the Library of Congress. At the age of 8, Buamah founded his nonprofit organization, Books Without Borders, Inc., driven by his passion to equip children with the essential tools to succeed.

In addition to his literary endeavors, Buamah has ventured into the world of production as the creator and producer of the inspiring TV show, "Nick's House." Beyond his creative pursuits, he finds joy in motivating his peers to realize their full potential and encourages them to dream beyond limits.

THE SKY IS NOT THE LIMIT
THERE IS NO LIMIT TO YOUR GREATNESS
NB
EST 2011

www.ingramcontent.com/pod-product-compliance
Lightning Source LLC
Chambersburg PA
CBHW050012040726
47599CB00014B/1342